The MAGIC TRIANGLE
South of the Teign Estuary

Deryck Seymour

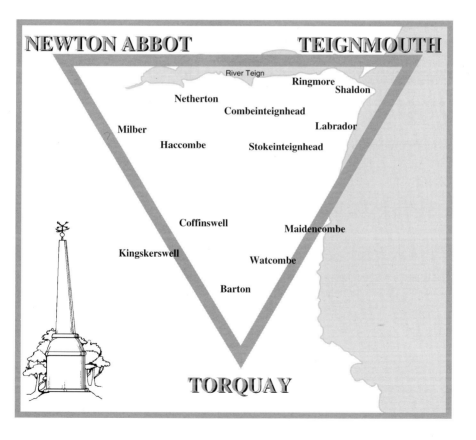

NEWTON ABBOT TEIGNMOUTH

River Teign

Ringmore
Shaldon

Netherton

Combeinteignhead

Milber

Labrador

Haccombe

Stokeinteignhead

Coffinswell

Maidencombe

Kingskerswell

Watcombe

Barton

TORQUAY

OBELISK PUBLICATIONS

If you enjoy this book, you may like to try some of our many other titles of local interest, which include:
Tales of the Teign, Chips Barber and Judy Chard
The Templer Way, Derek Beavis
Ten Family Walks on Dartmoor, Sally and Chips Barber
The A to Z of Dartmoor Tors, Terry Bound
The Great Walks of Dartmoor, Terry Bound
Torquay, Chips Barber
Dawlish and Dawlish Warren, Chips Barber
Also by Deryck Seymour:
The Ghosts of Torbay
The Ghosts of Berry Pomeroy Castle

For further details, please contact
Obelisk Publications, 2 Church Hill, Pinhoe, Exeter EX4 9ER
or telephone 0392 68556.

Acknowledgements
My thanks are due to the following people who have so kindly helped me in making the publication of this book possible: The Rev. C. M. Blunsum, Mr H. Bucklow, Theo Brown, Mrs Boyd, Canon G. Ruming and John Hopwood who so kindly gave of their time in providing transport when required, Mr and Mrs Deane, Mrs Fey, Mrs Geary, Mr S. Hook, Mrs R. Haywood, Mr M. Dowdell and the very cop-operative staff of Torquay Library, Mr J. Lawrence who so kindly read the script, Dr Robinson Thomas, the Rev. R. Southwood, the Curator of the Walker Art Gallery, Merseyside, Mrs P. Whiteaway and Mrs Edna White. I do apologise if I have inadvertently omitted any names.

Plate Acknowledgements
Chips Barber for pages 2, 6 and 25; Jerome Dessain & Co (Nicholas Toyne) page 10; Jane Reynolds pages 15 and 17; Mr Tozer page 30; Title page and Front Cover map by Sally Barber; Back cover photograph of Shaldon Beach by Chips Barber.

Bibliography:
"Devon" Arthur Mee; "Devon" N. Pevsner; "A Guide to Shaldon"; "Combat and Carnival" P. Carew; "Over the Hills" Keble Martin; "Smuggling in Devon and Cornwall" Mary Waugh; "The South Devon Hunt" Edward Tozer; "The Templer Way" Derek Beavis; "The Lost Village of Labrador" Calver; "The Churches of Devon" J. M. Slader.

First published in 1993 by
Obelisk Publications, 2 Church Hill, Pinhoe, Exeter, Devon
Designed by Chips and Sally Barber
Typeset by Sally Barber
Printed in Great Britain by
Ashley House, Marsh Barton, Exeter, Devon

AN INTRODUCTION TO THE MAGIC TRIANGLE

This little book is about the country around the south side of the Teign Estuary. It is kindly Devon at its very best, with tall hills, narrow lanes, and lush green pasture in its steep-sided valleys. The area concerned is contained within the sides of a rather irregular triangle. Get out your map and you will see at once what I mean, for it extends from Shaldon up the river Estuary as far as the Penn Inn roundabout outside Newton Abbot. It then heads for Torquay where it bears left on the outskirts of the town. At the roundabout at Hele Corner a left turn will put us on the final leg of the Triangle and take us back to Shaldon. You will find that each leg is about four miles in length, and the best of it is that in our Triangle there is no town. Instead you will see, for the most part, an undisturbed countryside. Shaldon has certainly grown in the last few years, but it still delights to call itself a village – and a village with a west-end, too, for in Ringmore it has a delightful suburb. Yet Ringmore is centuries older than Shaldon, having in its midst the church of St Nicholas which goes back, some say, to Saxon times. The Triangle contains some attractive villages such as Coffinswell, Combeinteignhead, the old part of Kingskerswell and Stokeinteignhead. Besides these are some delightful hamlets which have so much to offer in the way of cob and thatch. One thinks of Netherton, Maidencombe, Daccombe and many other out-of-the-way spots so full of charm. Then there are the long valleys or combes hidden among the rolling hills, each with an individuality all its own. There is a feeling of deep country in these enchanted places, and yet all the time we are never more than three or four miles from Newton Abbot or Torquay. By the time you've seen it all you will have come under the spell of this seductive countryside and be ready to call our territory a Magic Triangle.

If I were to be your guide I would take you into it by way of the Torquay–Shaldon road which begins at Watcombe – the south-east corner. Preferably I would choose the morning, for then the sun would be shining on cliff and sea with its greatest brilliance. The road at first climbs steeply with Brunel Manor on the left. This is a house with an interesting history which will be described later. At the top of the hill the road levels and a series of S-bends begin which continue most of the way to Shaldon. This is not the road for a nervous driver! At the very moment when the sea comes into view for the first time the driver daren't take his eyes off the road, for he has to negotiate steep gradients and continuous bends; but his passengers will be having a whale of a time enjoying the glimpses of the sea and unfolding panorama. The coast just here is surely unsurpassed in the south of England. Arthur Mee, a leading authority on the English landscape, described it as "the best Devon has to offer", and few would disagree with him. Not for nothing is one of the inlets on the shore below called Cherry Red Cove. What a contrast are these smiling red cliffs and fields to the cruel, hard, granite coastline of North Devon.

After climbing again from Maidencombe Garage and wriggling round some serpentine bends a welcome lay-by soon hoves into sight on the right hand side. On a clear day it is such a fine vantage point that it may be as well to pull in here and give the driver a chance to see the view. You are four hundred feet up now, and if you are lucky will see Portland Bill, which is over forty miles away to the east. Most of Lyme Bay is before you, though you cannot see its southernmost tip at Start Point. To the left lies Exmouth with the red cliffs of East Devon, whilst beyond them is the white coastline round Beer Head which continues into Dorset.

On resuming the road you will soon encounter the celebrated Labrador Bends. Below is the site of a lost village, once a den of smugglers. It is intriguing to consider how Labrador probably gave its name to the east coast of Canada, for many of the original settlers came from these parts. The road soon straightens and then it's all downhill to Shaldon. Teignmouth sea-front and the railway line which runs beside the sea, with its many tunnels and towering cliffs, are now in sight. After rounding a left-hand bend the first view of the Teign Estuary comes into sight. If you are lucky the tide will be in, and you will see before you what appears to be a lake of shining water half a mile wide. Shaldon is connected to Teignmouth by an iron bridge which is both ugly and useful. The serpentine road which we have been following has one last fling in a downhill hairpin bend, and if you can manage this one safely you will have arrived in Shaldon. The main street lies straight ahead, so take care if you decide to explore it, for you will have all the traffic from the bridge coming across your bows. To cross it needs courage!

The second leg of the Triangle begins by going in the opposite direction by way of Ringmore Road. Very soon you will pass Ringmore Towers on the right; this is a truly

delightful nineteenth century folly, and just beyond it you will discover what a truly delightful waterfront Ringmore has. The only trouble is that there's not enough of it. Once you have passed the Strand and climbed a short, twisting hill you will be out of the village and heading for Newton Abbot. But the river is never very far away, and those who live in the houses dotted along its bank are certainly to be envied. The first point of interest is Arch Brook Bridge, to the left of which is a sequestered valley leading up to Stokeinteignhead by way of a bridle path. Below the bridge a small creek opens onto the river where, in summer, there's always boating activity. After another mile or so there is a right-hand turn which leads to Coombe Cellars – formerly a smugglers' haunt and now a much frequented beauty spot on the river.

A few yards beyond the turning lies the attractive village of Combeinteignhead, with its neatly thatched houses and red church tower. The road bypasses the village at its northern end, proceeding next through Netherton – an alluring little hamlet nestling among steep hills. Here, on another day, we shall turn left to visit Haccombe, and right to discover Netherton House and Buckland Barton, which lie amid the tangle of narrow lanes between here and the river.

The road now climbs to its highest point of 282 feet, and here the wide expanse of woods and hills which surround the shining estuary come into view. The mile-long descent which now begins is noted for the fine sight which its beech trees provide in autumn. We now approach Newton Abbot through the newly developed estates of Buckland and Milber. As you wait at the traffic lights at the Penn Inn roundabout, keep your eyes open for Forde House which stands among the trees behind Penn Inn.

We do not enter Newton Abbot, for you will remember that I promised you no towns in our Triangle. This is not to say that Newton Abbot is uninteresting, but its charm needs seeking out. Baker's Park, for instance, is delightful, and can lead to a walk up the River Lemon, whilst Courtenay Park with its elegant Victorian villas, together with the stately houses on Wolborough Hill, compare well with anything Torquay has to offer.

The final leg of the Triangle begins with a left turn at the roundabout into the Newton Abbot–Torquay main road. There is at first a stretch of terraced houses built originally for railway staff. This is somewhat relieved by the church of St Luke, Milber, which has a central tower capped by a green pyramid. It is unusual in many ways and will be discussed later. The right hand side of the road offers a much more agreeable view with an open countryside composed of green meadows and distant hills. Kingskerswell is now soon reached, and here the road is thickly built up on both sides. Behind it is a maze of lesser roads and bungalows mostly built since the last war. The old and very attractive main street of the village still remains, however, tucked away from the rush of the main road with which it has nothing whatever to do. It lies away to the right and is not signposted, but it is worth seeking out for it extends down to a rather fine railway bridge (known locally as the "viaduct"). From its parapet you will be rewarded by the pleasant sight of the old church set among chestnut trees with a swiftly flowing stream beside it.

After continuing along the main road for a further mile or so the outskirts of Torquay are reached; but this lies beyond the green Triangle, and so a left turn must be firmly taken at traffic lights below Torbay Hospital, which will be seen on a hill to the right. Pass the Crematorium, go straight on through Hele village to the busy roundabout below. After a left turn here one is soon clear of the built-up area, and the trees and hedges near Torquay Golf Club soon appear. Press on and Watcombe soon shows itself. This is where we entered upon the Triangle. So having perambulated its boundaries we can now describe all the interesting things it contains.

SHALDON

"It's a good place to idle away a summer morning," says Dr W. G. Hoskins, author of that indispensable book *Devon*. How right he is, and what an excellent place it is to wile away a summer's morning!

But small though Shaldon is, there's much more to do and see than would occupy just a morning. By the time you've climbed to the top of the Ness, played a round of approach golf, visited the Shaldon Wildlife Collection and browsed around the shops you will be quite ready for some lunch. Now there is no difficulty at all at Shaldon in ministering to the inner man, for you can get anything from a snack to a ploughman's lunch – or a meal of several courses – yes, and the quality will be good. The next thing will be to walk it off and indulge in wandering round the truly delightful maze of narrow byways which await discovery behind the waterfront. Now Cornish seaside villages may have just as interesting a network of side roads to explore, but the villages there are usually perched on the side of precipitous slopes, so there will be steep hills or steps to negotiate, whereas at Shaldon it's just no trouble at all for the village is all on the level, and I guarantee that the stretch between the approach to Ness House and Ringmore Strand is as flat as the back of your hand. So there is quite a mile of easy walking here for the visitor.

The intricacy of the little streets behind the Strand at Shaldon has to be experienced to be believed, and it is quite easy to get well and truly lost. But it's all in a good cause, for all the time there are some delightful houses to notice; they are all of differing ages and sizes. Now you may be passing a cottage of cob and thatch whilst next to it may be a gem of a Georgian house; there a fantastic verandah and here a well-proportioned bow window.

2. Shaldon Bridge, Teignmouth

We have the river Teign to thank for all this level walking; you can read elsewhere how the tidal waters once swept over the site of Shaldon. Then after a very long period the river began to carve for itself a deeper channel on the Teignmouth side, depositing sand the while on the Shaldon side. This action is said to have been caused by waste deposit washed down from Dartmoor, when the tin streamers got busy up there. All this happened over five hundred years ago, and when the mud which built up was gradually drained, then it was possible to build. At first there would be just a few huts and it was not until the reign of King James I that Shaldon was mentioned by name. Later there began a vigorous fishing trade with Newfoundland which continued for over two centuries. Boats were built on this side of the river as well as at Teignmouth. Houses were built on the Strand for the fisherfolk and their families. They still stand today, and it is interesting to note how each has its piece of land on the opposite side of the road. This was for the laying out of nets and the stowing of fishing gear. The great challenge of the sea was there from the first for the men of Ringmore, and later of Shaldon; and the church registers of the surrounding villages show how many a sailor came from them too. They lived a hard, tough life, these mariners; in the spring they set sail for Newfoundland, and in the autumn they returned with their catch. During the winter they made good their boats and nets and were all ready for the next season. When the men were absent much of the farming was done by the women – yes, and fishing too. Celia Fiennes, when on a visit in the seventeenth century, noted in her diary the roughness of these women and their outlandish clothing. "Their dress is barbarous and their coat is pinned up in the shape of a pair of trousers, leaving them wholly naked to the knee," she wrote.

If the sea and the river drew men then, they still do so today but in quite a different way. The great difference, however, is that on this side of the river at any rate, the owners of the boats make their money from other peoples' pleasure and very little else. Just consider what fun you may have on the river today. There's sailing, water skiing, rowing, wind-surfing, and fishing of all kinds. There's plaice, pollack, mullet and eel for the taking; and I've heard it said that the Teign is the best river in the country for flounder. Then there are mussels, cockles and oysters which are best from the Salty; this is a considerable sandbank that appears at low tide just below the bridge. Live bait is available from local fishermen, and I'm told it's very good.

If you don't happen to want to fish then you can be taken out in a motor launch, or you may prefer a hire and drive boat. There are moorings here for boats of all shapes and sizes up to seventy feet, but plutocrats are advised not to bring a boat of ponderous tonnage up the river and expect the swing bridge to open up for them. This, I understand is not encouraged, and you might find a bill for £1,000 on your breakfast table as a result.

Bathing is not all that safe from Shaldon Beach because there is a five knot current with which to contend, depending on the state of the tide. So, by and large, it is better to go round to the Ness Beach where there are delightful sands which are ideal for safe bathing; and this can be said of all the coves and beaches between here and Watcombe.

Don't forget that the quickest and simplest way to Teignmouth is by ferry. The great advantage is that you can leave your car on the Shaldon side and don't have to bother about parking when you get to Teignmouth. Apart from winter weekends the ferry runs frequently every day. It's rather interesting to consider that it has been plying to and fro for centuries, and still uses the black and white colours adopted in Tudor times.

Very much in the centre of the village you will find The Green – indeed it's almost impossible to miss. Here the fishermen used to dry their nets. The surrounding houses are pleasant and sunny, and there is a clock tower memorial to the men of both wars. The Silver Jubilee of H.M. Queen Elizabeth II is commemorated by a map of the village set on a granite plinth in 1977. There are one or two small buildings of particular charm, such as the Wesleyan Chapel (now Methodist) of Georgian days in Fore Street. Its coloured walls of light blue, rounded windows and frontage walls not at right angles with the rest of the buildings are quite delightful. So also is the Roman Catholic Church on the opposite side of the road which is also a Georgian building, once Nonconformist.

It would be a pity if you went off to Teignmouth without exploring Ringmore which has an atmosphere all its own. The Strand is a conservation area, and the pleasant lawn and gardens here have been well laid out. Comfortable seats are provided, so this is a pleasant place to relax and admire the Estuary. Ringmore is not a place to walk around, guide-book in hand; it is a place to explore slowly on your own, without the promptings of other people. The visitor will be constantly rewarded by unsuspected charms and delightful houses of all periods. So I shall mention nothing specifically, but remind the visitor that this is the oldest part of the village. If you had sailed up the Estuary in mediaeval times all that would have been seen on the left bank would have been the little village of Ringmore, with its church of St Nicholas just rising above the rooftops. It was a Domesday manor and old houses yet survive. At that period there would have been as yet not a sign of Shaldon.

If the return journey is made via the Embankment, then on the right hand side are King George V Playing Fields. It is to be hoped that this green oasis will always be preserved and put to good use, for its position is extremely fine, with the river on one hand, the view upriver to Dartmoor in the far distance, and the tall hills surrounding.

St Peter's Church

All the while we have been walking along the Embankment towards St Peter's Church which now begins to dominate the scene. This is a building which dates from 1902, and since it is most unusual in style it is worth while crossing the busy road to Teignmouth to explore it.

Shaldon possesses only one building of size and distinction and this is St Peter's Church which superseded the old church of St Nicholas as parish church. The village had grown tremendously just before the turn of the century and the bulk of the population lived at the Shaldon end of the parish. So it was felt at the time that the more spacious new church should take pride of place as the parish church.

It was designed by Edmund Sedding who came from a family of distinguished church architects. The exterior from a distance appears long and low with no distinctive features. It certainly gives no promise of the quite spectacular interior. A tower was originally intended, and this no doubt would have been a splendid landmark from the river. Unfortunately it was never built owing to strong doubts as to suitability of the sandy river bank to carry its weight. Undistinguished as the exterior may be, one has only to open the door to step into another world – and one of great originality and beauty. J. M. Slader, author of *The Churches of Devon,* considers St Peter's to be one of the three finest churches built in Devon at the turn of the century, whilst the screen he deems the finest of its kind in the west country.

The varied stone and marble employed in the building make for a colourful interior which is seen at its best on a bright day. The church has been likened to a tunnel in stone, and the vaulted barrel roof of stone was inspired by one in Italy. There is also a stone altar and a stone apse of unusual style, lit by very narrow windows. The stone is of varied hues and came from places as far apart as Polyphant in Cornwall, Portland, Beer, Babbacombe and red sandstone from the Ness. There is an elaborate pulpit of marble with steps of alabaster. A feature of the church is the numerous carved figures, the largest of which is the figure of St John the Baptist, holding a clam shell which does duty as the font.

There are two splendid features in the church which should not be missed: firstly the richly carved marble communion rails of the Lady Chapel, which are decorated with lilies most delicately worked with exquisite effect, and secondly the wrought iron lectern which portrays a very active serpent. But the building is full of skilled work and one needs to visit it many times to absorb its full beauty. St Peter's is fortunate in possessing also a really fine organ, and during the summer season recitals by eminent players are frequent.

The south door is usually open.

Shaldon Bridge

It is hard for motorists of this generation to understand what a difficult county Devon was to traverse until the beginning of the nineteenth century. Its roads were traditionally bad, and in the middle ages sledges were used rather than wheeled traffic to negotiate the appalling highways. In South Devon, for instance, there was no good road over Haldon Moor to Exeter, so the only way north lay through Teignmouth, hugging the coast after crossing the river as best one could. At high tide it seems that passengers went by boat whilst their horses swam behind. At low tide it was possible for carriages to splash their way across.

This sort of thing was still going on at the beginning of the nineteenth century when Teignmouth and other small coastal towns began to expand; then the need for a bridge became of paramount importance. A Joint Stock Company was formed eventually, and by 1827 a wooden bridge had been completed. It consisted of 34 arches and was acclaimed as the longest wooden bridge in the country. It was built by Roger Hopkins, a civil engineer and mineral surveyor. It contained a swing bridge which opened in two parts, where vessels of three to four hundred tons could pass through the deep channel of the river. Its length was 1671 feet. The roadway was 24 feet in width, and the arches were of wood and iron. The outlay was about £2,600. It is recorded that Queen Victoria, then Duchess of Clarence, drove over it on her way to Plymouth soon after its opening.

It speaks well for the construction of this bridge that it lasted until 1931, when it was replaced by the present structure, which is mostly of steel. The old bridge did suffer one major disaster in 1838 when one of the sections collapsed. There is in existence a rare print which shows the span nearest Teignmouth falling into the river. This is carefully recorded as happening on Wednesday morning, June 27th, the swing section being the part affected. The cause of the accident was that one of the spars had been rotted through by shipworm. Fortunately no other spars were affected. The damage was quickly rectified and the bridge continued in use for another 93 years.

The present bridge is 1080 feet in length, and has 24 spans. Its width is 28'6" and the carriageway between kerbstones is twenty feet. The girders are carried on circular concrete piers. Like the old bridges it has a bascule at the Teignmouth end where the deep water channel flows. It is very seldom used, however. Recently pedestrians have been given greater safety by the construction of a concrete kerb with iron railings. Lorries of over 17½ tons are forbidden.

At first the Shaldon Bridge Co. owned the bridge, and it was built at a cost of £40,000. It was then a toll bridge – the return fare being 1/6; but in 1948 it was taken over by the Devon County Council and since then has been free of toll. The toll house still stands at the Teignmouth end, and if you chance to visit the "Chequered Lantern" in Fore Street you will see the original black and white lantern which was fixed to the front of the toll house, showing, when dark, where toll was to be paid. There is a rather fine milestone at the beginning of the bridge on the Shaldon side, and on the left hand side as you face Teignmouth. It is interesting because of its very precise measurements given so accurately in miles, furlongs and perches:

Torquay 7m 2f 4p
Brixham 15m 2f 2p
Dartmo 17m 5f 2p
Totnes 17m 0f 2p

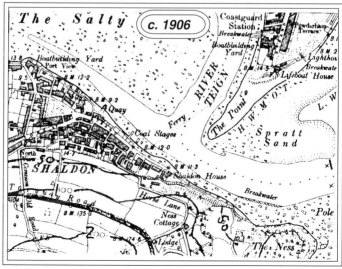

It was probably erected at the time of the opening of the bridge in 1827, when it would have been of decided use to coach drivers who were at first unfamiliar with this route. The bridge linked up with the new turnpike road to Torquay which was made at about that time.

The Ness

At the extreme end of the Teign Estuary, on the southern side, stands the Ness – a bold headland of red sandstone which rises steeply to its tip, very like a sudden crescendo in music. Once seen its unusual shape will never be forgotten, and certainly no mariner could ever doubt his position when the Ness hove in sight. Formerly a bare upthrust of land, it was planted with trees to mark the Silver Jubilee of Queen Victoria. When floodlit of a summer night the red cliff and trees take on quite an ethereal glow. The Ness estate, consisting of some 72 acres, belonged at one time to Lord Clifford, and his family used Ness House as a summer residence. It is now the property of Teignmouth Urban District Council who acquired it in 1949. Formerly gates blocked the end of Marine Parade; now, however, there is access to the whole estate. Drivers from Torquay will turn right at the 18-hole Approach Golf course and descend to the spacious carpark. Below this, in a dip, is Ness Farmhouse – a picturesque thatched house where Nell Gwynne is said to have stayed; but what she was doing so far off course is hard to imagine. The building seems old and may once have been just a barn.

Close by is the entrance to the Shaldon Wildlife Trust's grounds, where there is a pleasing collection of small animals and birds living happily among the trees. This is an altogether delightful little zoo and well worth a visit. A steep path on the right will take you to the highest part of the Ness, but you must bear left at the top of the rise. From here a steep pull leads to the summit of the promontory and there is an extensive view to admire. The right hand fork below represents the start of the cliff path to Babbacombe, and is a part of the Devon (South) Coast Path, linking up with the coastal path which goes all round England.

But before leaving the Zoo entrance area don't miss the entrance to a real smugglers' tunnel which has a lime kiln at its entrance. Its true purpose in times of yore seems unfortunately to have been forgotten, but it is known to have had another entrance in the cliff beside Shaldon House which is now blocked by fallen rocks. It is not possible to date the tunnel by its masonry for this has been much restored from time to time. The guess that it was constructed during the Napoleonic Wars does not seem very feasible as it would have given direct access from the Ness Beach to the village. Notice, however on the right hand side, and not far from the entrance, a refuge such as one sees in a railway tunnel. Its use would be for a man to step into when meeting oncoming traffic; so evidently horse-drawn traffic once came this way. It may have carried limestone from the beach to the kiln which had just been landed – yes, and smuggled goods as well. However that may be, this is a typical schoolboys' dream of a smugglers' tunnel, and if it wasn't, then it certainly ought to have been!

Ness House will be seen standing a little below the foot of the car park. A typical seaside Regency villa, it is now a hotel and restaurant. Shaldon is graced with quite a few such houses and this one, in its charming setting, is one of the best. In 1895 the house, and presumably the whole estate was purchased from Lord Clifford by Henry Forbes Julian (1861–1912), the famous metallurgist, and he stands out as one of the distinguished people to have lived in our Triangle. He set up his laboratory here, and being the great authority on cyanidation, was sought out by experts from all over the world. In 1902 he married Hester Pengelly, daughter of William Pengelly, the famous geologist who put Kent's Cavern on the map. The Forbes Julians moved to Torquay eventually, and in 1912 Henry, who was setting out on a visit to the Californian gold mines, was one of those unfortunate people who embarked on the ill-fated *Titanic,* giving his own life whilst trying to assist others to safety. His memorial is in Upton Parish Church, Torquay.

Cars may be driven from Shaldon along Marine Parade to the Ness car park, but owing to the one-way traffic system must drive out at the top of the car park, turning right at the Torquay Road and so returning to Shaldon.

Homeyard Botanical Gardens

In Homeyard Botanical Gardens Shaldon possesses a quite extensive open space on the steep slope above the village. The garden was the brainchild of Mrs M.L.K. Homeyard of Ness Cottage, who owned the land on which it is situated. The work was carried out in the years 1929/31 being designed by Thomas Rider. It was William Sears, however, the foreman in charge, who did the landscaping, and an Italianate stone seat commemorates his work. Magnificent views of the Haldon Hills, Teignmouth and the Estuary are obtained from the various terraces. There is an attractive folly in the shape of a castle where Mrs Homeyard used to entertain. It is situated on a level, terraced arboretum. There is a pond and rockeries planted with yuccas, cistus, phlomis, escallonia etc. Above the pond the coat of arms of the Borough of Southwark is mounted, for Mrs Homeyard had a business in Clerkenwell. She had various Cornish relatives who had well-known gardens, and it was with these in mind that this one was modelled. She died in 1944 and in 1950 Teignmouth Town Council purchased the gardens. There is an onward-going programme of tree planting, fostered by Friends of Shaldon Botanical Gardens.

William Newcombe Homeyard, her husband, perhaps qualifies as another person of note to reside in the Magic Triangle, for he produced and sold a famous cough mixture known as "Liquifruta". He and his wife are buried in Ringmore churchyard, and the word is on the tombstone, but spelt backwards "ATURFIUQIL". The story behind this is that when her husband died, Mrs Homeyard submitted a design for his tombstone to the local vicar, the wording of which extolled the virtues of "Liquifruta". The parson said it was not the thing to have a commercial on a gravestone so Mrs Homeyard later asked if she could submit another gravestone design, this time in Latin. Not wishing to show his lack of knowledge of Latin, the parson nodded sagely. This caused much amusement in the village, as the vicar was one of the very few in the village who didn't know that the "Latin" inscription was in fact "Liquifruta" spelt backwards!

St Nicholas's Church, Ringmore

The former parish church of St Nicholas, Ringmore, is a little hard to find for it lies back from the Shaldon–Newton Abbot road at the end of a short cul-de-sac on the right hand side. This will be found just where the road begins to climb after leaving Ringmore Strand. Shaldon and Ringmore comprise one parish known simply as St Nicholas.

The church is a charming little building of red sandstone set in a spacious, well-cared for graveyard. It consists of nave, south porch and bell turret. It has no tower, and though on the rising river bank, hides itself among tall hedges and trees. It was founded by Stephen de Haccombe c.1280, though some think this may have been the refounding of an older Saxon church. It is probably no larger now than it was then.

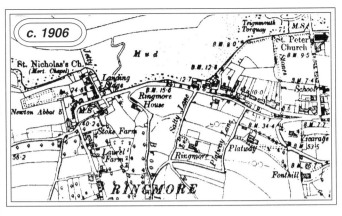

This little church has an atmosphere all its own and is well worth a visit. If locked the key may be obtained close by.

SMUGGLERS' PATHS

Wherever you go in the Magic Triangle stories of smugglers abound. The red cliffs along the coast between Petitor and Shaldon have at their feet an abundance of small, sandy coves which were ideal for beaching the kind of boats which smugglers used. There are about a dozen of these inlets where smugglers are known to have plied their trade. Their titles are hotly debated and it seems that local seafarers have their own names for them. Most agree on the names of the principal inlets such as the Ness Beach, Labrador or Maidencombe; but there is one inlet whose title must be quite indisputable and that is Smugglers' Cove which gives the hall-mark to the activities which went on there. Now quite a few of these little beaches have no paths or steps leading down to them, and so mounted patrols would be quite unable to reach smugglers in the act of landing their cargoes. But then neither could the pack ponies get down, and so human beings were the only means of getting the contraband goods up those formidable steeps. Men, it is said, could carry two kegs of brandy – one on their backs and another on their chests. After their long struggle to the top they must have been glad indeed to see the little pack ponies patiently awaiting them. Their hooves would have been padded with special leather boots so that their passing would be quite silent. The passage inland must have been fraught with danger for the excise men were provided with riding officers who were armed. Each provided his own horse and was certainly a foe to be reckoned with, for he could cover the ground at considerable speed. These officers doubtless lived with their ears to the ground, as it were, and the smugglers could never be sure that they hadn't got wind of their exploits. The risks they ran were therefore considerable, but then, so were the profits. They could buy tea, for instance, at 6d. per pound and sell it for six or seven times as much.

The smugglers would not have so much to fear from the local population, for most of the gentry would be only too pleased to buy a keg of brandy, and would but rarely lift a finger against a smuggler. The farming community would be of the same mind if they could afford to buy, whilst it is well known that the smugglers scared the locals off the road at night by putting about stories of ghosts on the roads they frequented. They are said to have resorted to dressing up as ghosts, and headless drivers were reputed to have been seen on the road between Maidencombe and Shaldon. The soft ridge roads around the Beacon and No Man's Land were ideal for a quick, quiet getaway inland, for they all had high hedges. So a string of pack ponies could even get away by daylight and not be seen, though moonless nights were doubtless preferred.

Certain of the inaccessible coves would be used as dumping grounds for a cargo – all the safer because it was so hard to scale the cliffs to reach it. Word would be passed as to where the coveted goods had been deposited, so they could then be collected at leisure. The actual smugglers would have long since made their getaway in safety, and it is possible that payment awaited them in secret hiding places along the coast. Labrador is said to mean in French "l'abri d'or" – the "shelter of gold". So perhaps it is not too fanciful to suppose that there was indeed a shelter or cache there for payment in gold which awaited the smuggler. Some bold spirits actually brought their booty upriver to Coombe Cellars if they chanced to know that the excise men were occupied in another direction. Whatever the hazards were, the stories which have come down to us insist that the inn at Coombe Cellars was the best known hiding place along the coast. Strategically it was in a strong position because the mounted officers in the days before the bridge was built could only cross the river at low tide; and even then they could not do it without being seen, and so the inn would always be alerted in good time.

At Labrador smuggling would seem to have begun in the seventeenth century when a certain Captain Trapp is said to have built himself a cottage there in 1630. He soon became a full-blown smuggler himself and started a thriving trade from Labrador. A small village at the base of the cliff resulted; but when smuggling no longer paid, about the middle of the nineteenth century, it became deserted and fell into ruin. Trapp's cottage survived, however, and in the twentieth century became incorporated in a hotel which was built there. It was known as "Labrador Bay Hotel" and included several chalets built alongside. No road was ever made to lead down to it, so it could only be reached by walking down four hundred steps, or else taking a boat from Shaldon. Goods were got down by an aerial ropeway. Much money was spent on advertising, as a

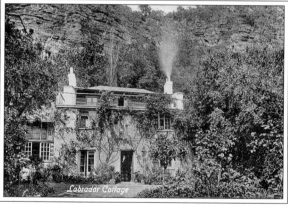

Labrador Cottage

glance at local newspapers of the 1930s demonstrates. Some quite famous actors who sought peace and quiet stayed there, including Tom Wall and Mabel Constanduros whose names the older generation will recollect. But it all came to a tragic end one night in 1938 when the hotel went up in flames. On account of its position the Fire Brigade could not reach it, and firemen are reported to have tried carrying water down in biscuit tins and buckets. It was all in vain, for the building was completely gutted. So ended the last link with the smuggling community at Labrador.

It has come down over the years, apparently by word of mouth, that there were in the district various hidey-holes for smuggled goods. It is related in several books on the subject that at the old Post Office in Park Road, St Marychurch, there was a secret cavity under the hearthstone, another at Higher Rocombe Farm, where there was a trapdoor in a ceiling which led to a secret room; and another was at Court Farm, Maidencombe, whilst at Coombe Cellars inn, where the bulk of the goods seem to have been taken, there was a secret room where as much as seven tons of tobacco could be stored. I have recently visited all these places and have not been rewarded by finding anything of interest. More amazing is the fact that the memory of their former existence has quite died out. Only at Park Road could Edna White tell me of a secret room beneath a courtyard at the back of her house which was formerly entered from the property next door. The entrance is now unfortunately blocked and there is no means of getting in today. The row of terrace houses here are known to have had space under their roofs for the storage of smuggled goods, as there were no dividing walls between the houses. An outside staircase against the wall of the end house formerly gave access to would be customers.

The sequence of events on a smuggling expedition would appear to have been somewhat as follows: first the illegal cargo would be landed at one of the many coves on an auspicious night. It would next be man-handled up the cliffs to the waiting pack ponies. When these had been loaded up both men and beasts would set out for their respective destinations. I see such places as Maidencombe, St Marychurch, Rowcombe and Coombe Cellars as larders for the local population. All the stories which have come down to us insist that the latter was the principal store-house, so from there it was that contraband goods were distributed in all directions. If ponies kept to that side of the river they could radiate all over the south of Devon without having to touch a town. Those heading north went across the river at low tide, which could be done in those days, knowing full well that excise men could not surprise them from the river. Only on the far shore might an ambush have been laid, but no doubt a system of signalling would have been in use. The trade seems to have flourished for at least two hundred years, reaching its peak in 1782. In that year Commissioners of Excise spoke of the existence of twenty five armed vessels of up to one hundred tons, with crews of up to twenty men which carried goods to the Exeter area. It was estimated that during the past three years 1,248,000 gallons of brandy and 80,400 lbs of tea were smuggled into South Devon. Newfoundland fishing boats would bring back with them rum, tobacco, salt and wine. On their return journey they would illegally export wool, arms and military stores.

Although the coming of the railway caused the collapse of the trade, yet it still continued sporadically; there was for instance a sale of smuggled goods at Brixham in 1867 which had been found on rafts in Torbay and at Babbacombe. Rum, brandy and Geneva are mentioned. Previously the lugger *Fly* had been caught with contraband and the cargo auctioned. Indeed, for those living along this coast smuggling seems to have had a fatal fascination. It was regarded almost as a sport or past-time, whilst schoolboys' tales of smugglers have always proved irresistible. The crime was not all that bad, people thought, and in fiction it was always the smuggler who was the hero – never the exciseman. He was always the villain! Yet no less a person than Dr Johnson in his forthright way described smugglers as "wretches who, in defiance of justice and the laws, import or export goods without payment of customs."

That wonderful stretch of coast may seem very quiet to you as you walk along the cliffs thinking, perhaps, of all those smuggling exploits of not so long ago, really. Do you ever wonder, as I do, whether it might not be possible that even now, if you watched closely on a dark night, you might not see something looking rather like a boat coming in on the tide? Could it be? Well, just turn to the local papers for October, 1991, and you will read how £4.5 million pounds worth of cannabis was smuggled into Anstey's Cove, and 12 men were arrested. Later on £80,000 worth was trawled up there by a local fishing boat! It certainly makes you think!

Five and twenty ponies,
Trotting through the dark
Brandy for the Parson,
'Baccy for the Clerk;
Laces for a lady, letters for a spy,
And watch the wall, my darling,
While the Gentlemen go by.
"A Smugglers Song"
Rudyard Kipling

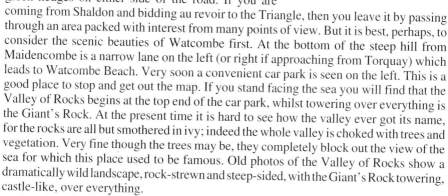

WATCOMBE

Watcombe is situated at the southern tip of the Triangle. If it is approached from Torquay this is where one can say goodbye to the town, with pleasant green hedges on either side of the road. If you are coming from Shaldon and bidding au revoir to the Triangle, then you leave it by passing through an area packed with interest from many points of view. But it is best, perhaps, to consider the scenic beauties of Watcombe first. At the bottom of the steep hill from Maidencombe is a narrow lane on the left (or right if approaching from Torquay) which leads to Watcombe Beach. Very soon a convenient car park is seen on the left. This is a good place to stop and get out the map. If you stand facing the sea you will find that the Valley of Rocks begins at the top end of the car park, whilst towering over everything is the Giant's Rock. At the present time it is hard to see how the valley ever got its name, for the rocks are all but smothered in ivy; indeed the whole valley is choked with trees and vegetation. Very fine though the trees may be, they completely block out the view of the sea for which this place used to be famous. Old photos of the Valley of Rocks show a dramatically wild landscape, rock-strewn and steep-sided, with the Giant's Rock towering, castle-like, over everything.

This is probably the best place to warn would-be rock climbers that the Giant's Rock should be left alone; it is composed of crumbling sandstone and therefore decidedly dangerous.

The path down the valley takes you round the coast to Maidencombe via a goat's path with glorious coastal views. The road from the car park leads down to Watcombe Beach, but on account of the extremely steep gradient is for pedestrians only. The little beach is sandy and offers a pleasant enough place to pass a summer's day. There is a refreshment kiosk and toilets. The road is crossed by the Coastal Path on its way from Petitor and Babbacombe to Maidencombe and Shaldon.

On returning to the car park there are two rather fine Victorian villas to notice. On the left is Watcombe Hall and on the right Watcombe Court. Both, strange to say, were lived in by people of note in their day and were centres for unusual undertakings. Both were planned by I.K. Brunel whose work at Watcombe Park will be considered later. Until 1877 Watcombe Hall had an interesting resident in Colonel Ichabod Wright, and later came Sir Horatio Davies, Sheriff of London and Middlesex, and also Lord Mayor of London. But the house had to wait until the 1920s before it really hit the headlines, and then it became the HQ of Cairns Torquay Film Co. A large film studio, measuring 60' x 50' x 30' was erected beside the house, and the films *Unrest* and *Where the Rainbow Ends* were made there. The strong light and clear atmosphere of South Devon were said to be conducive to good production. The local papers predicted a new Hollywood for Torquay, and in 1921 were boasting of the most up-to-date film studios in England. I don't think that any one really believed in this venture, and sure enough enthusiasm soon waned and languished. There was an attempted revival as late as 1946, but it all came to nothing.

As we tour the Triangle we shall find that quite a few celebrities have resided there. For instance from 1927/31 Watcombe Hall became the home of the famous Australian-born sculptor, Sir Bertram MacKennel. He was the first Australian to be knighted and the first to be elected to the Royal Academy. With Lutyens he executed the national memorial to King Edward VII in St George's, Windsor, a portrait of Queen Alexandra in Sandringham Church and the tomb of Sir Redvers Buller in Winchester Cathedral. He also designed the Coronation Medal of King George V, and the obverse of the new coinage for that reign. The Dictionary of National Biography describes him as "A brilliant all-round sculptor and master of his craft – particularly in his treatment of marble with poetical imagination and peculiar elegance of style."

Opposite Watcombe Hall stands Watcombe Court, formerly Watcombe House, and

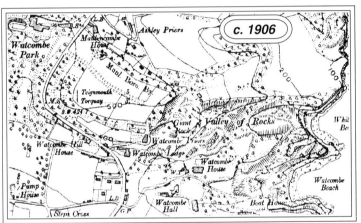

c. 1906

the venture undertaken here through a chance find proved far more lucrative than the film fiasco on the other side of the road. There lived here in 1867 a certain Mr Allen who was the retired headmaster of Dulwich College. In that year he discovered a rich vein of clay on his property whilst a well was being dug. It proved to be far superior for the manufacture of terra-cotta than anything hitherto discovered. It was eventually to be dug between the house and the Shaldon road, and in 1864 Watcombe Terra Cotta Clay Company was founded. Between 1870/71 they erected a Pottery. Now art pottery at this time was the order of the day, and the success of the Watcombe venture was assured when Baroness Burdett-Coutts gave Queen Victoria a pair of Watcombe Water Bottles as a birthday present. Other terra-cotta potteries soon sprang up in the neighbourhood, each adhering to its own distinctive patterns. Watcombe was noted for its kingfisher design and the now very collectable "Cottage Ware". Nevertheless it is sad to record that few of the potteries survived for long after the Second World War; one by one they went out of business and today none are left. However, it all began with the digging of a well at Watcombe House!

One other fine house of this period still stands, and that is Watcombe Lodge, once Watcombe Villa. It is on the same side of the Shaldon road as the others. Here the Brunel family resided periodically whilst the Watcombe Park project was getting under way. It is now time to explain about this project and how Brunel, the great engineer, came to be involved in it, thus qualifying as the next celebrity to have connections with our Magic Triangle.

Brunel and the Watcombe Park Project

The story of Watcombe Park, now known as Brunel Manor, is a fascinating one which relates to one of the greatest engineers which the world has ever seen – Isambard Kingdom Brunel (1806–1859). His great achievements need no rehearsing here, but strangely enough his story converges with our travels in the lovely stretch of country behind Shaldon, for in the year 1847, when he was occupied with the construction of the South Devon Railway, he was so impressed with the beauty of the locality that he decided to make it his home. None of the Torquay villas or surrounding country houses were evidently good enough for him; he wanted to create a beautiful park at the centre of which would stand a splendid mansion for his eventual retirement. He finally selected land on the southern slope of the steeply rising hills behind Watcombe. At the head of a narrow valley, and at a height of very nearly five hundred feet, he resolved to build his house. It was, in those days, rather a forbidding site, open to practically every wind that blows; but with the help of William Nesfield, a well-known tree expert and landscape gardener, he ringed it round with a cunningly planted tree belt. Some of these trees still stand doing their duty as a windbreak.

Brunel also planned an avenue to extend along what was to be the main drive to the house. It was to begin just below Great Hill, Barton (which in 1849 he bought for £10), and run in an easterly direction to the house. The cellars of the house were built under the great man's supervision and the rockery and water garden laid out; but in 1859, he suddenly died at the age of only fifty three.

This blow naturally brought all work to a halt, but not before certain other work had been done under his supervision. This included the embankments to the roads on the estate which were faced with stone in the same style as his railway embankments. Brunel had also diverted the old Torquay–Shaldon road, which went right through the middle of his property, into the new turnpike road. He had also designed a timber bridge which joined the two parts of the estate. It was made on the same principal as many of his wooden railway bridges and the work was carried out after his death by his son, Henry.

But the prime mover in the Watcombe Park project was no more, so it is hardly surprising that the Brunel family felt that they could not carry on building the splendid house which was to have been the crowning joy of Isambard's eventual retirement. They therefore sold Watcombe Park with its unfinished house to John and Robert Vicary. They did not hold it for long but sold to James Roper Crompton, a wealthy paper manufacturer, and it is to him that must go the credit for completing the house on Brunel's foundations. Now the original designs had been drawn up by William Burn – one of the most exclusive of country house architects. His design for the front elevation hangs in the hall for all to see. Just who was responsible for the eventual building is not clear, but at any rate the house which was finally built owed more to the French style than to anything Italianate. It is peculiar to say the least. Some parts of it are on a very large scale – the cathedral-like front door, for instance and the main staircase. The best points, perhaps, are the Elizabethan-style chimneys so tastefully interspersed with red brick. A large hall was later built on, running eastward from the main house. Its purpose was for lavish entertainment.

Mr Crompton extended the estate considerably by taking in the Valley of Rocks at Watcombe, running southward to Moor Lane and northward to Claddon Lane – five hundred acres in all. In 1876 the whole estate was bought by Colonel Ichabod Wright and he was followed by a Mr James Peck. Later came Sir John Edwards Moss; it was he who built the annexe now known as the Rodenhurst Room and changed the name of the house to Roby Hall. Sir John eventually sold to Frederick James Lund in 1923; he sold a good deal of land to Torquay Corporation, including the public park to the south of the estate. In 1932 it was acquired by Thomas Crossman, a timber merchant. He quickly resold to the Holiday Fellowship who ran it as a Christian Holiday Home until the outbreak of war in 1939. From 1940–45 the house was occupied by the evacuated Stockwell Teacher Training College. Finally in 1963 it came into the hands of the Woodlands House of Prayer Trust, who carried out much extension work in the 1980s.

For most of the year it is run as a Christian Conference Centre, but in the summer it functions as a hotel as well. It would be difficult to imagine a more peaceful spot in which to relax, with its panoramic views of Torbay and tranquil surroundings. There is a swimming pool, tennis courts and children's play areas. The name of Roby Hall has long been forgotten and at some time was superseded by the prouder title of Brunel Manor. And so the name of the great engineer who loved Watcombe so dearly has been perpetuated for us as a reminder of his outstanding genius.

STOKEINTEIGNHEAD

This is a really attractive village which lies in the heart of one of the long combes which are so typical of this countryside. It is easily reached from the Shaldon–Torquay road by turning off at Maidencombe Garage. A long, winding combe begins here at about three hundred feet, just above Maidencombe which, with its pleasant cove, is also worth a visit. The road descends gently to the village, after which it forsakes the valley, and if you want to follow it to the river you must do so on foot, for the last mile wends its way through fields, reaching the river at Arch Brook Bridge.

Visitors naturally want to know the significance of the "Teignhead" tacked on to the names of Stoke and Combe. "Surely," they say, "Teignhead is far away on Dartmoor?". In this case some historians consider that "Teignhead" is a corruption of "Ten Hides", signifying that in the Middle Ages a particular lord of the fee owned ten hides of land in which the villages lay. Just who he was is obscure at the moment. This seems a reasonable enough explanation.

The winding lane descends at first through the hamlets of Higher and Lower Gabwell where there are some delightful cob and thatch cottages. After a little over a mile we reach Stokeinteignhead where the road levels out. The village

c. 1906

has a charm all its own, and there are some attractive buildings of all ages for your camera. Everything is smiling and well tended. The red sandstone church of St Andrew stands to welcome you on a steep slope just above the rooftops. As a village church it is most satisfying, with its imposing west end tower and clock. The interior is light and spacious, and it is easy to see that this was once a cruciform church, but that aisles were added later. The arcade is unusual because the sturdy red pillars, with their boldly carved capitals seem a size too large for the delicate arcade which they carry. No doubt the arcade is later in date.

The church's most remarkable treasure is its screen, for it is quite unlike the usual Devonshire type, being earlier in date – late fourteenth century. In the Sanctuary, on the north side, is another treasure, this time a fine brass depicting a fully vested priest. Pevsner considers it to be c.1375, which makes it the earliest brass in Devon. Much later is a charming little heart-shaped brass hidden by a mat in the Nave. It commemorates Elizabeth Furlong, 1641, shows a skull and cross-bones and has an inscription in early French.

Notice also the wrought iron font cover which is decorated with gilded flowers copied from illustrations, in the famous *Concise British Flora in Colour* by Keble Martin (see under St Luke's, Milber). The south porch has a particularly fine sandstone doorway with its old door intact. The village stocks survive, too. On your way from the church notice the old granite cross base on the left hand side.

Below, and also on the left, is the Church House Inn. It is a particularly well cared for example and has thick cob walls and a thatched roof. In the bar is the original open hearth of massive proportions, and above it some stalwart beams. All this was part of the former Church House. The village boasts a shop or two besides the pub and in the season you can eat here. The houses are in varying styles and represent many different epochs in the history of the village – yet all blend happily together. This is a good starting off point for walks, and surrounding are a number of earthy lanes undisturbed by traffic which makes walking pleasant.

COMBEINTEIGNHEAD

The combe which begins just below Great Hill, Barton, meanders down the Rocombe valley, narrowing considerably at Charlecombe, until at Combeinteignhead the village is closely hemmed in by hills on both sides. It is a comfortable, homely spot with cob and thatch mingling happily with later styles of architecture. Opposite the church lych-gate the first building to catch one's eye is an unusual one of red sandstone blocks with fine oak doors and mullioned wooden windows. You will be told that in its time it has been many things. Be that as it may, it began life as a Church House, and a facsimile of a grant of land for its site is to be seen hanging near the doorway. From it we learn that it was built in 1530 on land known as The Bery by John Bourghchyre, lord of the manor. In return prayers were to be said for him each Sunday from the pulpit. At the moment this interesting little building is a well-stocked art gallery but it has come through bad periods when it became almost ruinous.

Just below it a charming garden was constructed to mark the present Queen's Jubilee. Set back from the road and agreeably planted with trees and flowering shrubs it is just the place to sit and contemplate on a summer morning. The pleasant stream on the other side of the road soon leads down to Coombe Cellars and the old salt marshes. The name is said to derive from "salters" and not cellars.

The tower of the red sandstone church (All Saints) watches over the village but in this case the church stands alone, for the pub is further up the road. It is approached by an attractive lych-gate. The building in plan resembles Stokeinteignhead church. It must at first have been cruciform and later aisles were added. It is light and friendly with delicate carving displayed in the screen.

Every church seems to have a special point of interest, and here it is the lively carving of the bench ends in the north transept. Depicted here are saints, two wild men, a fool, an archer and a fox taking a goose. There is also a tomb chest in the east wall of the transept, and squints in both transepts which look through to the high altar. The memorials in the north transept commemorate members of the Hockmore family of Buckland Barton which will be considered later. A fine Norman font stands at the back of the church, looking as though it were carved yesterday, so little has the stone deteriorated in seven hundred years. Its decorative palmettos and bands closely resemble those at nearby Coffinswell, and it is tempting to suggest that they were the work of the same mason.

Coombe Cellars

Coombe Cellars, just below the village deserves a paragraph to itself, for it is the most frequented spot on the Estuary. The inn must always be linked with the smuggling which went on in days of old. The section "Smugglers' Paths" relates all about that side of its story. The Coombe Cellars Inn is today a very popular place to eat, and too much cannot

be said for its perfect situation on the river. Much boating and fishing goes on there in the season and there is also a yacht marina. The Templer Way passes through here; it is named after James Templer (b.1722). He owned granite quarries at Haytor, getting the granite away from the moor by means of a granite railway, and then by canal to the River Teign. Here it was floated down the river by barge to Teignmouth for export. The "Way" follows the whole course from Haytor to Teignmouth, and the last section of it stretches from the head of the Estuary to Shaldon. There is no actual path here, however, and hikers must follow the shore line, being wary all the time of the state of the tide. At low tide all is well, but at high tide walkers will get driven inland. Coombe Cellars is a good vantage point from which to ascertain the state of the tide before going on towards Shaldon.

Netherton

It is less than a mile from Combeinteignhead to the hamlet of Netherton which lies on the road to Newton Abbot. Up a hill and down a hill and you're there. If you're driving a car, mind you don't pass it before you've arrived! These secluded hamlets which are dotted about the Magic Triangle are usually worth a stop and a second glance. It may be that there's just a rippling brook to see, with a pleasing bridge and an old-world cottage that takes your fancy, but these sequestered corners all go to make up the closely-woven tapestry of which this countryside is composed.

At Netherton is the left turn to Haccombe, but what you may well miss unless you're looking for it is an unusual stone seat, set back a little from the cross-road on the right hand side. Beside the seat when I visited it were well-tended trees and shrubs and also a poppy wreath. A card attached read: "The people of Haccombe with Combe remember the fallen. Nov. 10th, 1991". The story behind this is to be found on the rather unusual inscription on the back of the seat:

Both these young men were owners of the adjacent estates of Haccombe and Netherton whose boundaries adjoined just here. Possibly in life they were great friends. How different would have been the subsequent story of each estate had they lived.

Haccombe and the Carews are written about elsewhere, so let us turn right close beside the seat and follow a single-track lane which in less than half a mile will bring us to Netherton House. It is delightfully situated on the river bank just above Coombe Cellars. The house is surrounded by fine woods and is late Victorian, built in 1887 with red sandstone from a nearby quarry. The architects were the Penwills of Combeinteignhead, who were a family of masons and built several excellent houses in the neighbourhood. It is not a large house by any means, but it has an air of quiet grandeur and dignity enhanced by its position and superior design.

The rough-edged sandstone is tastefully interspersed with a light yellow brick which is particularly successful in the chimneys. The main façade has one very interesting feature and this lies in the fact that it is not in a straight line, for the east wing turns south at an obtuse angle. This apparently was a later addition, built on to contain two large mullioned windows which came from Sulgrave Manor in Northamptonshire. The result is most satisfactory, and the large room concerned catches far more sunlight and has a better view of the grounds than it otherwise would have done. The house was clearly built for comfort and gracious living. Note how it firmly turns its back on the river so that it gets all the sun. Most people would have thought that the prime view down the Estuary was the first consideration, but this was ignored, and the frontage looks out on level lawns and handsome trees which effectively screen it from the bitter winds that sweep up the Estuary. Buried in its windbreak Netherton House is well sheltered. All this was designed by the first owner, Arthur Reynell-Pack who built the house. He was Squire Pack to his tenants, for he was lord of the Domesday manor of Netherton. His father who had married into the Reynell family (who in 1610 had built Forde House) adopted their name in addition to his own, when his wife brought him the manor of Netherton.

Squire Pack seems to have been very much of a personage in his own locality and to have ruled his estate in feudal style, rather like Sir Walter Carew at Haccombe in the previous century. Every morning before breakfast he would mount his horse and, with his bulldog Judy at his heels, ride round his estate to see that all was well. He must certainly be regarded as one of the outstanding people of our Triangle and one who had plenty of money and knew exactly what to do with it.

He owned a splendid steam yacht called *Nerissa* which older people well remember. He went on annual cruises in it, bringing back rare and exotic trees with him from foreign climes; some are still living in an arboretum which he planted near the house. Among these is a fine cork tree which is still in good shape. When he embarked on a voyage his tenants would assemble on Netherton Point to wave goodbye and be there to welcome him on his return. He would moor the *Nerissa* just below the house where he had built a jetty and boathouse. At Christmas he would send his coachman down to Netherton with presents for all the tenants' children, and at Easter they were invited up to the house to collect Easter Eggs which he had hidden about the lawns for them.

Squire Pack had one son by his second marriage who was always known as Master Tommy. The squire died in 1937, but his son only enjoyed his inheritance for three years, being killed, as we have seen in 1940. To complete the Netherton House picture of that era Septimus Carruthers, the butler, must not be forgotten. It is remembered of him that on his day off he always sported a flower in his buttonhole, wore a bowler hat and carried an ebony cane.

The Squire is buried at Combeinteignhead a few yards from the west end of the church. There is a nicely shaped granite cross and the remains of a kerb on which is inscribed "Arthur D.H.H. Reynell-Pack, 1860–1937" A scant enough memorial to one so well known and respected in his lifetime.

Sadly, "Master Tommy" had no heir, and the fine house has been put to many uses since his tragic end. It was first an evacuee centre, then a guest house for foreign students, next a hotel, and finally the offices of a business firm. Now it stands empty, and one can only hope it will soon be acquired by a family who will delight in both the house and its beautiful surroundings.

Buckland Barton

There were several Domesday manors adjoining Combe, which itself was one. Among them were Ringmore, Stoke, Rocombe, Netherton and the most westerly Buckland Baron to give it its old name, "Barton" being a corruption of "Baron"; but in Domesday it was just "Boclond". The old manorhouse now to be considered has been in its day something far grander than a mere barton farmhouse, for it was the home of the Hockmore family whose interesting memorials in the church at Stokeinteignhead have already been considered. Its extensive lands came down to the river on the north side, adjoined Netherton to the east, Milber to the south and the Aller Brook below Penn Inn to the west. Apart from this house and Court Barton there are no other remaining manor houses in our Triangle. There are, nevertheless, quite a few worthwhile farmhouses such as Teignharvey and the Rocombe farms, but this is not quite the same thing.

Here we have what was once a considerable L-shaped house, and I do not doubt that it is the successor on the same site as the first Saxon manor house. The façade which greets the visitor is impressive. It is a solid, dignified building in part three storeys in height. It contains three fine tiers of granite, mullioned windows, the ground floor example having no less than eight lights. The first floor has five lights, but with charming recessed arches, and the second floor four lights with similar arches. The shaping of these lights is more than usually skilled in workmanship. The main supports of the roof are original, and all over the house is much good panelling. There are also some decorated plaster ceilings. The house was most probably remodelled in the fifteenth century and would be a typical hall-house of the period; but since then there has been so much change and alteration that it is hard to get a clear picture of what the mediaeval house was like. Nothing much remains in the way of old outbuildings; I remember hearing some thirty years back of a barn, demolished c.1930, where a fresco of a religious scene had been uncovered. It was unfortunately destroyed by ignorant workmen.

Visitors should note the fine chimney which dominates the front of the house. It is of sandstone but has lately been stuccoed over and so does not look quite so attractive as formerly. One feels that this is an exciting old house where there is much more awaiting discovery.

Milber Down Hillfort

Athwart the Newton Abbot–St Marychurch road stands a splendid example of an Iron Age hillfort of the South-western type. It is completely bisected by the road. As this is a very old ridge road one cannot help but wonder which came first! The earthwork stands on the western side of a considerable hill, so that whilst the outer bank on the north west side is only 270 feet above sea level, yet the opposite bank on the south east side is four hundred feet up.

It is unfortunate that this fine earthwork cannot be seen in its entirety, because the half to the north of the road is entirely covered by vegetation; therefore apart from old air photographs the visitor can only get a lopsided view of it. An excavation was undertaken here in 1937 by Frank Cotrill, but it was never regarded as anything more than an interim undertaking. A report of this was published by the D.A.E.S. but the Second World War put a stop to further work at that time. Nothing further has ever been undertaken, however.

It was found that the defences of the main part of the camp consist of three banks with an outer ditch. The spacing between the banks is wide, and it is this characteristic which makes this earthwork a typical southwestern type such as Lady Fox defined in 1952. The additional space, she considered, provided ample protection for flocks and herds. This suggested a pastoral rather than a military use of the hillfort. Milber, therefore did not fulfil the same role as, say, Hembury in East Devon which is sited on a steep spur and whose ramparts are much more formidable. This hillfort provided protection for both man and beast from sudden coastal invasions or landings on the Estuary.

Fragments of pottery were found on the bottom of the second ditch. Most attractive of all were the bronzes which consisted of a recumbent deer $2\frac{1}{2}$ inches long, a duck of the same length, carrying a disc in its beak, a bird $2\frac{1}{2}$ inches long with a tail, a pair of wings probably belonging to the bird and a ball $\frac{7}{16}$ of an inch in diameter. These may be Gallo-Romanic work of the first century AD. They may be seen in Torquay Museum.

The only other earthwork in the Triangle was a small one said to have been on the summit of Great Hill, Barton. It was unfortunately destroyed when the reservoir was made and no record seems to have been made of it.

ST LUKE'S, MILBER

On a bank above the busy Newton Abbot–Torquay main road, and about half a mile from the Penn Inn roundabout, stands the unusual church of St Luke, Milber. Its style is quite off the beaten track, and J. M. Slader in his book *The Churches of Devon* states that "it may justly claim to be the most exciting church built in Devon since the Reformation." Its story is even more bizarre, for it is interwoven with the life and fortunes of a country parson who achieved fame in his 89th year. Until 1965 the Rev. Dr William Keble Martin, apart from his pastoral work at Coffinswell, Torrington and later Combeinteignhead was quite unknown. But in that year he happened to publish a best seller, *The Concise British Flora in Colour* which made him world-famous as a botanist, and adds yet another person of note to have lived in our Magic Triangle. The Duke of Edinburgh in the foreword described the book as "the triumphant outcome of sixty years meticulous and devoted study, research, note-making and exquisite workmanship." To add to this Dr Martin produced designs for postage stamps in 1967. The 4d stamp had four designs, the 9d one, and the 1/9d one. But all this was a side line – a hobby, if you like, for he was as well a hardworking parish priest. When the old GWR built rows of terrace houses for their staff at Milber he found a sudden influx of some two hundred people on his doorstep as it were. He immediately began work among them, although they were not strictly speaking in his parish. It was not long before a wooden church was built, but it was obvious that a permanent church should be built. Then a remarkable thing happened for Dr Keble Martin one night had a vivid dream in which he saw an unusual church which had three naves all focussing on one altar but from different angles. They were surmounted by a central tower. He became quite obsessed with his dream, feeling that he had been shown what the new church should be like. Fortunately he had a brother who was a competent architect. He assured him that his idea was quite feasible. To cut a long story short, the new church was built exactly in accordance with the dream. It was to be 1,000 inches long, 1,000 inches wide and 1,000 inches in height, and so it is. In its early days it was known as "The Dream Church". The result is a cruciform church with a central tower. The two extra "Naves" are at forty five degrees to the central nave, and are both extended beyond the crossing to form a Lady Chapel on the south side and a Sacristy on the north. The two triangular spaces formed between the three "naves" are filled with a font on one side and a statue on the other. All the furnishings are of an excellent standard and there is an air of lightness and spaciousness which pervades the whole building. St Luke's was opened in 1963, and it is a happy thing to record that Dr Martin lived to see the day – indeed he married again when well on in his eighties. He was honoured by Exeter University with an honorary D.Sc. degree in 1966 retiring after seeing Milber on its feet, and went to live at Woodbury where he died in 1969 at ripe old age of ninety two.

St Luke's is well worth a visit. The key is available at the house opposite.

HACCOMBE

Take a look at the map of our Triangle and you will see that Haccombe is towards the northern end of it, a mile or so south of Combeinteignhead. Look again and you will discover that it is on the way to nowhere, for it consists of just a church and a large house at the bottom of a valley; it is in fact one of the steepest of the combes, with hills all around it which rise to four and five hundred feet. To get there from Shaldon follow the road to Newton Abbot as far as Netherton – a snugly situated hamlet beyond Combeinteignhead – and there turn left. The lane climbs a little and then flattens out, and you will soon find yourself in the Haccombe valley with its green parkland all around. There us no village here today but there once was, and an old map shows that it was quite extensive. The final stretch consists of a driveway which leads to the church and Haccombe House. This is journey's end, for you can go no further. The last time I visited this favoured spot was in spring. The lawns before the house had just been mown for the first time since winter and glistened in the sunshine, whilst the well-tended churchyard was a mass of daffodils, hyacinths and a host of other spring flowers.

The first object of note is a fine old granite cross which stands near the railings; it is incised with a cross near the top of the shaft and was discovered nearby at Buckland Barton Farm at the beginning of the century. It was set up here as a First World War memorial. The little red sandstone church beyond has an immediate appeal simply because of its remote rural setting. It consists simply of nave and north aisle. There is no tower, but a bell-cote over the west gable in which there hangs one of the oldest bells in Devon, for it dates from c.1290. So it has rung out over the valley week by week for over seven hundred years.

The church is dedicated to St Blaise, and there are only two other churches in England so dedicated. He is the patron saint of woolcombers, and was martyred by beheading in the year AD 316, but not before his skin had been lacerated by wool combs. The church was founded in 1233 by Sir Stephen de Haccombe in thanksgiving for a safe return from a Crusade. Two generations later his grandson enlarged it in 1328 by adding the north aisle.

Perhaps the main interest of the interior lies in its tombs of which there are several. The large effigy on the north side of the Sanctuary should be the founder, Sir Stephen de Haccombe, whose crossed legs show that he was a Crusader. A giant of a man, this, if the figure is life-size. A great rarity is a heart burial, and in this case the effigy is little more than two feet in length, and depicts a small boy clad in armour. The figure is of alabaster, and thought to date from the fourteenth century. One authority describes this as the finest of its class in the country. Other effigies are those of the founder's wife and their daughter, Cicely, in the north chapel and Sir Hugh Courtenay on an altar

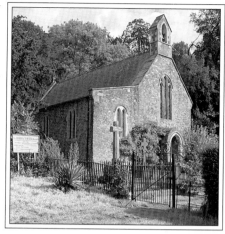

tomb of 1425. Four more effigies lie in the north aisle in specially prepared alcoves beneath the windows. They are spanned by relieving arches which go right through the thickness of the wall to reappear on the outside of the wall.

Among other treasures are the four brasses. They are well described in the church brochure and are all memorials of the Carew family who followed the de Haccombes as lords of the manor. They span a period of two hundred years.

Of great interest are the ancient tiles of which there are about four hundred. Some were made in Exeter, but others have designs unique to Haccombe, and the kiln where they were fired is thought to have been nearby at Aller. There are also blue and green tiles from Spain which have Moorish designs, and green, glazed tiles of the early sixteenthth century from Normandy.

The stained glass is worth careful study for there are considerable amounts of sixteenth century Flemish glass pictures set among later glass. The old and the new blend happily, and the various colours add much to the beauty of the little building, whilst letting in a good deal of daylight.

Another item of interest is wood from the *Mary Rose* which has been worked into the head of the processional cross. The *Mary Rose* was the pride of King Henry VIII's navy. One day she keeled over before his very eyes just off Southsea Castle. This was a major disaster, for besides losing the ship over four hundred men were drowned. The Haccombe connection is that Vice-Admiral Sir George Carew was one of those to be drowned. In 1982 the ship was raised, and the "Mary Rose Trust" gave two small pieces of wood to Haccombe Church in memory of Sir George who had worshipped there over four centuries ago.

After 102 years of existence a strange thing happened to St Blaise's Church. Hitherto simply the domestic chapel of the lords of the manor, it was in 1332 raised to the status of a Collegiate Church, and endowed with five priests and a Rector, known as an Archpriest. A college for them was built close by, but all memory of its whereabouts has long been forgotten. It continued until 1543 when it was suppressed, but the Rector of Haccombe still retains the title of Archpriest; moreover the Bishop of Exeter has no jurisdiction over Haccombe, which is directly under the Archbishop of Canterbury. A similar case in Devon exists at Bere Ferrers.

Be sure not to leave Haccombe without looking at the old horseshoes nailed to the outside of the south door. Evidently the complete set of four were there once, but now there are only one and a half! A delightful legend is attached to them. In the days of yore a Carew and a Champernowne laid a wager as to which of them could swim his horse farthest into the sea at Torre Abbey Sands. All went well until Champernowne's exhausted horse could swim no more and began to sink. Carew's horse swam to the rescue so valiantly that both horses and their riders reached the shore in safety. As a token of gratitude it was decreed that Carew's brave horse should work no more, in token whereof his shoes were removed and affixed to the church door. But then again horseshoes nailed to a church door were said to ward off witches, so choose whichever story appeals to you the most!

Haccombe House

Turning now to consider Haccombe House, we are confronted with a late Georgian mansion of red sandstone; it is dull but dignified. Peter Carew writing in *Combat and Carnival* says of it – "The great sandstone mansion flaunts its ugliness down the undulating park." Blunt and to the point, certainly, but it really is surprising that when the Carews decided to pull down old Haccombe Hall they did not build themselves something much more striking. Considering their high standing in the county one would have expected an outstanding house in that splendid setting.

The most notable of the Carews to live there during the mid nineteenth century was undoubtedly Sir Walter Carew whom we must now introduce as one of the famous people to live in the Triangle. He was a typical foxhunting squire with a great zest for life and unbounded energy. His ideas were sometimes eccentric and often alarming as, for instance, when he blocked up the windows of the servants' quarters so that they should not waste time by gazing out of them. Another version of the story is that it was done to avoid paying window tax. There must at that time have been much of interest to see out of those windows in his day. In a house such as that there would have been constant activity in the hunting season with the going and coming of guests and their horses. Then there would have been shooting parties bringing good company at the end of the day. It was a grand life then if you had plenty of time and money! He, of course, kept his own pack of hounds and was a dedicated huntsman. Fortunately he kept a diary of his hunting exploits which makes good reading. A saying of his which has come down to us is "Time is wasted on women which you can give to hounds." This is reputed to have been said to Lady Fortescue when out hunting!

I like best the story of a winter's day when the huntsmen were driven home by inclement weather and Lady Carew had just arrived home from an afternoon call. On alighting from her carriage she was astonished to hear strains of music coming from the church. On proceeding thither what should she see but Sir Walter rehearsing next Sunday's music with the servants. Not to be thwarted by the weather, as soon as he had dismounted, muddy, wet and begrimed, he had rounded up the servants and chased them all into the church for a rehearsal. What a rare picture that would have made, with Sir Walter in his top boots and hunting pink conducting his servants whom he had just extracted from their warm kitchen and put into the freezing church. Thus they sang away a dreary winter's afternoon. There was certainly a good side to domestic service in those days – a hard life it may have been, but they were well housed and well fed and hadn't a care in the world. Indeed the last of the servants have told how, during their youth spent in service, they had had endless fun whilst living with a good family.

Now Sir Walter had other interests beside hunting, and one was yachting; so during the summer months he competed in all the local regattas. When his yacht *Beatrice* was being designed he said to the builder, "None of your infernal engines in her, mind. I want fresh air and not to be smoked out by steam and soot. It may do for the Queen and that German fellow, but not for me." He once took *Beatrice* for a trip up the Baltic, visiting Russian ports. According to his daughter, "Papa, of course, does not speak any language but his own, nor would he ever think of doing so." However, he seems to have made himself perfectly understood by those "damned frog-eating foreigners" as he called them. Actually he delighted them by giving huge dinners which lasted several hours and were prepared by Gaston, his French chef, whom he had bribed to leave the Imperial Hotel at Torquay.

Shooting only played a minor part with Sir Walter, although Haccombe with its sunken vales and precipitous hills provided some of the best in the west. He is reputed to have grumbled when in 1842 income tax was 7d. in the pound, and said it made a difference of £500 a year to his income.

But whatever else Sir Walter did he always came back to his hunting and in the winter of 1831/32 he recorded 93 days hunting. In those days it was possible to cross the river at low tide, and at the end of a long day he often cut across, hounds and all, near Netherton. An old man called Arthur Owen related in 1901 how he once saw Sir Walter and hounds cross just above Shaldon Bridge. He himself records in 1839, "through Lyndridge across the river at Netherton Point," and again "Over Humber Moor to the river at Pleasure House. Fox crossed but tide too high for us."

Peter Carew describes him as something of an oaf, but I see him as far better than that, for he had the respect of the whole county. An old rogue he may have been, but he had an infectious joy in living and knew how to enjoy life at Haccombe. He died in 1873, but the excellent photographs of him preserved at the church bring him and his family very close to us. I never cease to wonder at the excellence of the photography of those days.

His stately home after going through many vicissitudes has finally been made into flats, and there amid peace and seclusion dwell some fortunate people – one cannot but envy them their lot!

Forde House

Forde House stands a very short distance beyond the Penn Inn roundabout in the direction of Newton Abbot; it can be seen on the right hand side of the road lying back from the road in its own grounds. Strictly speaking it is just outside the south-west corner of the Triangle, but for once we will overstep the boundary to pay a call, for this fine house is too good to miss when we are so close.

It was built in 1610 by Sir Richard Reynell, who had recently acquired the manor of Wolborough, and evidently thought he should build himself a house worthy of the occasion. It is a late example of the Elizabethan style of E-shaped house, with attractive rounded gables, mullioned windows and stately chimneys. The interior is famous for its graceful plaster ceilings (which are generally considered among the best in Devon) and good panelling.

The house has seen the visits of two monarchs, for this was a house where Charles I was received and welcomed, but where Prince William of Orange was received but not welcomed. Charles seems to have visited first in 1625 and later during the Civil War. On the first occasion he knighted the two nephews of Sir Richard, Richard and Thomas. On this visit there were prepared for the banquet 1,000 mullet, 54 whiting, 4 salmon, 7 peel, 7 dories, 26 plaice, 26 sole, 48 lobsters, 550 pilchards; as for birds there were 69 pullets, 14 capons, 112 chicken, 40 ducks, 6 geese, 37 turkeys, 69 pigeons, 92 rabbits, 4 teal, 3 peahens, 1 barnacle, 268 larks, 2 seagulls; meat included 6 oxen, 5 muttons, 2 veals, ribs of beef, chines, sides of lamb and gammon. The drinks, of course, were well looked after: 2 hogsheads of beer, 1 barrel of canary, and 35 quarts of white wine.

When Prince William of Orange came in November, 1688, Forde House had passed into the hands of the Courtenay family. Sir William Courtenay, the owner at the time, was, like most of the country gentry, greatly embarrassed by the Prince's arrival. He did not know whether to back him or to remain loyal to King James II. It seems that Sir William bolted, leaving the Prince to entertain himself; but another version of the story is that he feigned sickness and went to bed. It is also not absolutely certain that the Prince slept the night at Forde House, for some say that he spent it with his men, getting what shelter he could from the banks of the old prehistoric camp on Milber Down.

The mansion remained in the hands of the Courtenay family until 1936. Since then it passed through various vicissitudes until it finally was acquired by Teignbridge District Council whose offices now occupy the building.

It is interesting to record in passing that the scene portrayed in the well-known historical picture "And where did you last see your father?" by W.F. Yeames depicts a room in Forde House. The young lad being questioned would have been the son of Sir Richard (2) Reynell. I well remember meeting James Yeames, then a man of sixty who had been portrayed as the boy in the picture. It was a chance meeting in a railway carriage; we got talking and the conversation touched on Devon and eventually Forde House. He then mentioned the picture and his part in it. He was a nephew of the artist, whilst the little girl was his niece and James's cousin. The tenseness of the atmosphere produced by the picture is masterly. What would the boy answer? Would he give his father away? The picture was at one time popular in school history books and that is where I first met it.

DACCOMBE AND COFFINSWELL

" 'accombe, Daccombe an' Coffinswell –
All begins with 'a'."
(Old Devon saying)

Daccombe and Coffinswell have been close neighbours for centuries and both were Domesday manors. They are surrounded by a range of horseshoe-shaped hills which rise to as high as five hundred feet. It is the steepness of these hills which made both of them difficult of access in the past, and has helped to protect them from the intrusion of that odd bungalow or two which can so easily mar a rural landscape. Daccombe lies at the head of a combe two miles or so in length which gives splendid peeps of Dartmoor, and stretches toward Kingskerswell. Daccombe itself is little more than a hamlet, with two or three farmhouses, a handful of thatched cottages and unpretentious houses; but how charming it all is! The valley is fairly free of traffic and this makes walking pleasant.

Until recently Daccombe could boast the remains of a mediaeval chapel which stood opposite Manor Farm, lying back from the road. Consisting of the east gable only and a part of the south wall, it is mentioned in a charter of 1225 (Exeter Cathedral Library 2084). It belonged to St Marychurch, and in my book *Torre Abbey* there is further mention of it. At the time of my researches old people still referred to it as "the Chapel". Not one stone remains upon another today, however.

A mile or so to the south-west, but more up in the hills, you will find Coffinswell. It is a well kept village of special beauty in spring when its banks and verges are ablaze with daffodils. There is much beautifully maintained cob and thatch building, and the village boasts a church and a pub, "The Linnay". Its rather lugubrious name is easily explained, for the family of Coffyn acquired the old Domesday manor of Welle in days of yore, so Coffyn's Welle it became.

The surroundings of the church were at one time of great charm; it literally stood in the farmyard of Court Barton, the former Courthouse of Torre Abbey and whose Canons owned the manor of Daccombe, and a considerable acreage in Coffinswell until 1539. The farm buildings, with their thatched roofs, were all well maintained in the 1950s as a photo in *Torre Abbey* clearly shows. But over the years, with changes of ownership, the buildings became neglected and fell into decay. For many years the farmyard was a pitiful sight, but now the ruined buildings have been cleared, a house has been built in the north-west corner, and there seems to be a grand opportunity to preserve the old farmyard as a well laid out open space with lawns, trees and gardens. Immediately west of the church there still stands most of a former U-shaped building – probably the old tithe barn of St Marychurch, whose perquisite Coffinswell Church was until 1913. A cider press and roundhouse stood on the far side. The building is now being restored as dwellings.

One old building which has weathered the changes in fine condition is Court Barton. There are four handsome mullioned windows of granite in the courthouse, which is a wing running south from the main building. There is a spacious cobbled courtyard entered by a fine granite doorway. Here the Canons would receive their rents and conduct all business. The present owner has lavished much care on the house just when it was beginning to fall into decay.

St Bartholomew's church, though scarcely a mile from a busy main road, has the atmosphere of a remote country church. It is surrounded on the south side by a sunny churchyard which contains an old granite cross of moorstone. If you are energetic enough to climb the church tower you will be rewarded by a fantastic view of Dartmoor and the intervening countryside.

At the back of the church are some pattens affixed to a screen. They protected your feet from the good, red mud when you crossed the farmyard.

Not so long ago Coffinswell had a remarkable Rector in the Rev. Dr Keble Martin – another of the renowned people to live in the Magic Triangle. He was author of the *Concise British Flora in Colour*. Much of the work on this book was achieved during his stay at Coffinswell. He has been discussed more fully under Milber and the Dream Church.

KINGSKERSWELL

And so we come to the last village in the Magic Triangle, hoping that it has cast its spell upon you and that you will visit it again. It is possible to drive through Kingskerswell on the busy Newton Abbot–Torquay main road and see nothing of interest whatever. A pub or two – a petrol station or two and acres of bungalows and small houses which have sprung up between the two wars, and that's about it. But you have yet to find the old village, and this is quite hard to do, for it lies on a different level to the main road. If approaching from Torquay, fork left when the bridge comes in sight, and you will quickly land in the middle of a nineteenth century village street with the shops on the right.

Even then you must find the older village street which was cut in half by Brunel's railway, which arrived in the 1840s. This forks left from the present street and runs steeply downhill to Daccabridge – an old-world packhorse bridge with a low parapet. If you feel like wading in the stream you will see inscribed on the west side:

This Bridg was repard

By Ye COUNTY IN 1693

There are two old properties beyond, and then the road ends abruptly, cut in two by the railway, and until recently by Kingskerswell railway station. Note how beyond the railway the old main street continues as though nothing had happened. This is Yon Street where there is quite a lot to see in the way of old houses. The United Free Church, too, with its pointed gables and trim garden adds much to the atmosphere of this old-world street.

Follow now the nineteenth century main street, which, after a level stretch, descends steeply to Brunel's bridge and railway station site. The former consists of seven arches and is known locally as the "viaduct", thus demonstrating how highly the villagers of 1846 thought of it. It is so well constructed that it deserves more then a second glance. The station was once a hive of activity before the days of buses. At the end of the viaduct stood a tall three-storeyed building, and to buy a ticket you entered at street level to be greeted by a fast closed door with "Stationmaster" inscribed thereon. Hurrying past this in case the great man himself should appear, you descended by a steep staircase to the next floor where was the Booking Office. It was at this point that one always heard the train coming. Hastily grabbing a ticket and dashing down another flight of stairs, you emerged breathless onto the up platform just in time to see the train pull out. To catch a train from the down platform was even worse because after buying your ticket you had to climb up to street level again, walk the length of the viaduct and then run down about forty steps to the train. Obviously it was very easy to miss a train at Kingskerswell, and to add to your misery, collected on the bridge, could be a crowd of jeering youngsters enjoying the sight of perspiring grownups missing their trains.

Now the up platform boasted a signal box where dwelt a very matey signalman who was always ready to discuss the wonders of his geraniums; but the down platform completely eclipsed its neighbour by boasting a truly remarkable gents' loo. Its shape was most peculiar, its designer having begun with a rectangle but attached to this semicircular ends. It was of solid iron and had formidable spikes all round the top. Was this freak of platform furniture designed by the great Brunel himself in a whimsical moment, or was it a standard piece of equipment? Certainly I have never seen another and wonder if it ever won a place in a Museum. The ladies had their retreat in the basement of the station building amid great dignity. All too many country stations vanished under Beeching's axe. What a loss that was, for each had its own characteristics and added much to the local scene.

Kingskerswell in bygone days was a small market town. If you stand on the viaduct you can get quite a good idea of where it stood. Before you, and in the centre of the picture, stands the old Parish Church of St Mary, whilst beyond the graveyard are the ruins of the manor house which old maps marked in Gothic type as "Castle". Adjoining the churchyard on the south side is a long, low thatched building which by its size and shape suggests an old Church-house. On the other side of the road, a few yard further on, stands Pitt House, a well-restored cob and thatch house where good food can be had. But a very old inhabitant could remember when it was an inn – the "Seven Stars". Then on the other side of the church a few yards down the road is Whitpot Mill, whose overshot millwheel is still preserved. So with the old village street just behind us, and doubtless a few cottages in between, it can be seen where the nucleus of a small market town stood before the railway came.

It is worth pausing for a moment on the viaduct to admire the view of the old church with its surroundings made so pleasant by fine chestnut trees and the babbling brook which washes the churchyard wall. I like the name of Brookador which is attached to this part of the village. Both church and graveyard are well kept and a delight to visit. The tower, with its attractive stair turret, will be the oldest part of the exterior and should date from the early part of the thirteenth century. But the founding of the church will be far older, for there is mention of a Saxon chapel at the time of the Domesday Survey which belonged to St Marychurch. The present building is light and pleasant with large windows. The unusually large east window which dominates the church is attractive in every way, and into the stained glass are worked fragments of mediaeval glass.

The arcades are of different periods, the south of red sandstone being the older. The later north arcade is of Beer stone. In the north aisle are three effigies which lie beneath the windows; they are thought to be of fourteenth century date. There is a short south transept, and beneath the window some blank arcading of the Decorated period. The top of this has been mutilated to admit the later window. It is possible that this formed a background to a vanished monument where once the effigies lay.

Panels of the base of the old rood screen remain for us to see. Look at the south end and you will see how at one time it did duty as a sideboard or cupboard. No one seems to know when the church managed to retrieve it from secular use. Usually the main entrance to an old church is on the south side, but here the reverse is the case, and the impressive north porch has a parvise, a stoup and pebble paving dating from 1722. All this suggests that this was the main entrance and that the little town was adjacent. In the porch the old stocks are preserved and are unusual in that they have seven holes. The reason for this is the fact that in the middle ages whenever a church was dedicated to St Mary, the Seven Stars associated with Our Lady were commemorated by an Inn close by whose sign would be the "Seven Stars"; stocks with seven holes instead of six would also be found. Here we have both. It is now for the reader to hunt out other instances of this phenomenon. Totnes springs to mind with its parish church of St Mary and the Seven Stars Hotel, but I wonder where the stocks are hiding!

Close to the eastern boundary of the parish, and situated on the high hills to the north of Torquay, stands Barton Hall, at a height of nearly four hundred feet. It is on the old ridge road which runs from Kingskerswell to Barton Cross, leaving the village by Fluder Hill. The house is at the lower end of the same range of hills on which Brunel Manor stands, but in style is a generation earlier. Its foundation stone was laid in 1837. The well-known architect, E. W. Gribble, designed here a charming and elegant mansion in the the mock-Tudor style so popular at the time. The view over Torbay and the surrounding country is uninterrupted, and Barton Hall is well worth a visit on that score alone. It was built by Henry Langford Brown whose family had for generations been squires of Kingskerswell, formerly dwelling in the now ruined house beside the church. Squire Brown was a great yachtsman and it was one of his quirks that whenever he sailed into Torbay he fired a canon. This would be heard at Barton Hall, whereupon his carriage would immediately set out to pick him up at the harbour and drive him the three miles home.

The family continued to reside until the outbreak of the Second World War, whereupon the house was taken over first by the Fire Service and later by the Civil Defence. After the war the family never took up residence again and the house was sold, first to some Torquay business men and finally to Sir Fred Pontin. It is now run as a Chalet Hotel, but in spite of the chalets, numerous additions and car parks the old house still manages to dominate the scene. Its pleasing proportions, clock tower, sharply pointed gables and Gothic chimneys are still a delight to the eye. What fun Gribble did have with his dummy chimneys, narrow windows and magnificent porte-cochère. It was there that the canon finally came to rest when sailing days were over.

The house was destroyed by fire in 1862, and the efforts of the horse-drawn fire engines are graphically described in Pontin's "History of Barton Hall," obtainable at Reception. Meanwhile the spacious grounds and their many amenities are there for visitors to enjoy. Amongst other things are golf, tennis, squash, archery, swimming, bowls and, perhaps best of all, a dry ski slope where you can become proficient before tackling Switzerland. And all the time, below you, stretching away into the distance, is the glorious prospect of Torbay. The old house stands as a splendid reminder of a family which was loved and respected by Kingskerswell folk for many a generation.

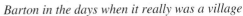

Barton in the days when it really was a village

If you come out of the gate and turn right you will soon be at Barton Cross on the outskirts of Torquay; from there, as the crow flies, it's only a mile to Watcombe and Brunel Manor – and that is where we first entered the Magic Triangle. So here I say goodbye to my patient reader, hoping that his appetite for its beauties has been whetted and that he will visit us again. So for him it will only be "au revoir".